FIRST PEOPLES

IROQUOIS

VALERIE BODDEN

CREATIVE EDUCATION ✕ CREATIVE PAPERBACKS

Published by Creative Education and Creative Paperbacks
P.O. Box 227, Mankato, Minnesota 56002
Creative Education and Creative Paperbacks are imprints of
The Creative Company
www.thecreativecompany.us

Design and production by Christine Vanderbeek
Art direction by Rita Marshall
Printed in the United States of America

Photographs by Alamy (The Keasbury-Gordon Photograph
Archive, Niday Picture Library, Photo 12, Stock Montage, Inc.),
Corbis (Corbis, David Muench, Tarker), Getty Images (Boyer/
Roger Viollet, Matt Champlin, Popperfoto, Science & Society
Picture Library/SSPL, Marilyn Angel Wynn/Nativestock),
Shutterstock (Ellika, Miloje, Emre Tarimcioglu)

Library of Congress Cataloging-in-Publication Data
Names: Bodden, Valerie, author.
Title: Iroquois / Valerie Bodden.
Series: First Peoples.
Includes bibliographical references and index.
Summary: An introduction to the Iroquois lifestyle and
history, including their forced relocation and how they keep
traditions alive today. An Iroquois story recounts how the
world began.
Identifiers:
ISBN 978-1-60818-903-8 (hardcover)
ISBN 978-1-62832-519-5 (pbk)
ISBN 978-1-56660-955-5 (eBook)
This title has been submitted for CIP processing under
LCCN 2017940105.

CCSS: RI.1.1, 2, 3, 4, 5, 6, 7; RI.2.1, 2, 3, 4, 5, 6; RI.3.1, 2, 3, 5;
RF.1.1, 3, 4; RF.2.3, 4

First Edition HC   9 8 7 6 5 4 3 2 1
First Edition PBK   9 8 7 6 5 4 3 2 1

TABLE *of* CONTENTS

PEOPLE OF THE LONGHOUSE

The Iroquois included people of many American Indian NATIONS. They lived in the northern part of what is now New York. Many lived in Canada, too. They called themselves *Haudenosaunee*. This meant "People of the Longhouse."

 Northern New York's lakes and mountains were home to Iroquois groups.

The Iroquois lived in longhouses. These were long buildings. The frame was made of bent trees. It was then covered with tree bark. Many families lived in each longhouse.

 Fires burned in pits down the middle of the longhouse to warm the home.

IROQUOIS LIFE

Several families made up a clan. The oldest woman of each clan was the clan mother. She chose men to lead the clan. These men talked to all clan members. Then they made decisions.

 Men like White Head (above, left) and Pau Puk Keewis (right) were tribal leaders.

roquois women farmed. They grew corn, beans, and squash. They gathered wild fruits, vegetables, and nuts.

 Children worked alongside their mothers and grandmothers to farm.

Men hunted ducks, geese, and deer. They fished in nearby rivers. They went to war with other tribes, or groups.

 Men hunted with bows and arrows from the time they were young boys.

IROQUOIS CEREMONIES

The Iroquois believed a Creator made the world. They held many CEREMONIES. In some, they wore masks. These were to scare away bad spirits.

 Some ceremonies were meant to heal people from their illnesses.

ON THE MOVE

SETTLERS arrived in Iroquois lands in the 1600s. The Iroquois traded with them. But the settlers brought new DISEASES. Many Iroquois died.

 Explorers from Europe made agreements with the Iroquois to set up trade.

I n the 1800s, the Iroquois were forced to live on reservations. These were areas of land set aside for American Indians. Some reservations were in New York. Others were in Wisconsin and INDIAN TERRITORY.

 Models of longhouses can still be seen in parts of New York.

BEING IROQUOIS

Today, many Iroquois still live on reservations. Some speak the Iroquois language. Others play the Iroquois sport of lacrosse. They keep their TRADITIONS alive.

 The French renamed the centuries-old Iroquois baggataway game "lacrosse."

AN IROQUOIS STORY

The Iroquois told stories to explain how the world was formed. In the beginning, the world was covered with water. Skywoman lived above the water in Skyworld. One day, she fell from Skyworld. Muskrat dove underwater to bring up a scoop of dirt. She put it on Turtle's back. It spread to become the whole world. Skywoman landed on the soil. She planted seeds. And the world began.

GLOSSARY

CEREMONIES ⇥ special acts carried out according to set rules

DISEASES ⇥ sicknesses

INDIAN TERRITORY ⇥ part of the United States that was set aside for American Indians; it is now the state of Oklahoma

NATIONS ⇥ specific groups of American Indians, often led by their own government and sharing a common language and traditions

SETTLERS ⇥ people who come to live in a new area

TRADITIONS ⇥ beliefs, stories, or ways of doing things that are passed down from parents to their children

READ MORE

Fullman, Joe. *Native North Americans: Dress, Eat, Write, and Play Just Like the Native Americans*. Mankato, Minn.: QEB, 2010.

Morris, Ting. *Arts and Crafts of the Native Americans*. North Mankato, Minn.: Smart Apple Media, 2007.

WEBSITES

Iroquois Nationals
http://iroquoisnationals.org/
Learn more about the sport of lacrosse and check out pictures of the Iroquois Nationals team in action.

Learning Longhouse
http://i36466.wix.com/learninglonghouse
Learn more about Iroquois art, sports, and more.

Note: Every effort has been made to ensure that the websites listed above are suitable for children, that they have educational value, and that they contain no inappropriate material. However, because of the nature of the Internet, it is impossible to guarantee that these sites will remain active indefinitely or that their contents will not be altered.

INDEX